Compliments of
Mr. and Mrs. George W. Headley

THE HEADLEY TREASURE
OF BIBELOTS AND BOXES

THE HEADLEY TREASURE
OF BIBELOTS AND BOXES

With a Foreword and Notes by

GEORGE W. HEADLEY

and an Introduction by

MARVIN C. ROSS

OCTOBER HOUSE INC · NEW YORK

Frontispiece: JEWEL FANTASY WITH PORTRAIT OF GEORGE HEADLEY

This *trompe-l'oeil* portrait of the author was painted in egg tempera by
Siegfried Reinhardt, in 1958.

Library of Congress Catalog Card Number 65-29280
Copyright © 1965 by George W. Headley
Printed and bound by Clarke & Way, Inc., New York
Color separations by Magnagraphic, Inc., Lexington, Kentucky
Designed by Bert Clarke

To Barbara Whitney Headley

Contents

"*The word jewel is significant. It was applied to precious stones and precious metals because they have been used from the earliest stages of civilization to commemorate and signalise human joy. Jewels have played a large part in the worship and adoration of the divine; how some of the most famous gems in history originally shone as the adornment of the images of deities, and how they were robbed by conquering captains of alien faith and used by them as a symbol of their pre-eminence among mortal men.*

The jeweller's craft is one of the oldest practised by man, and through its profoundly human significance, it was brought to a higher pitch of excellence at an earlier period than any other art. It has persisted through the generations, and the museums of all civilised nations. Its loveliness increases; it will never pass into nothingness."

from *The Art of the Jeweller*, by Francis Stopford

Foreword

Lay not up for yourselves treasures upon earth, where moth and rust doth consume, and where thieves break through and steal.

FROM THE SERMON ON THE MOUNT

Many times I have been asked how I came to create my jeweled bibelots and boxes. There have been many reasons. Years ago I wished to form a collection of the jeweler's art in gold—a few great examples from each of the ancient cultures. As a beginning, who would not be proud to own the following objects:

> The gold helmet of Mes-kalam-dug from Ur, c. 2700 B.C.
> The rythons and amphore from the Greek Treasure, 400–300 B.C.
>   from Panagurichie in Bulgaria, discovered in 1949
> The Etruscan gold bowl at Praeneste, late seventh century B.C.
> *St. George and the Dragon* in gold, jewels, enamel, German, 1590 A.D.
> The gold monstrance by Arfe, sixteenth century
> The *Winter Egg* by Fabergé, nineteenth century

But these were impossible to obtain: the gold helmet was in the British Museum; the Greek treasure in the museum in Sophia; the bowl from Praeneste in the Victoria and Albert Museum; the St. George in the Schatzkammer Der Residenz in Munich; the monstrance in the Cathedral of Toledo; and the *Winter Egg* in the collection of Bryan Ledbrook. Collecting great examples was really difficult, and the awareness of each country of its "national treasures," which are not allowed to be taken out of the country, did not make it easier.

I had always designed the usual jewels to be worn: necklaces, rings, and bracelets. From these my interests moved on to designing bibelots, *objets de vertu*, and boxes for my clients. The best of materials and workmanship were necessary, and it was my good fortune to know the greatest jewelers working in gold and precious stones today. The small group of craftsmen in New York gave interpretation and "life" to my work, while for enamel and beautifully made boxes my jeweler friends in Milan were invaluable. Other ideas of mine were wonderfully executed in Athens and Rome. The great art of the master jeweler is almost extinct, due largely to mass production methods, castings, and the unwillingness of younger men really to master this difficult and painstaking profession. Only a few of the older goldsmiths are working in the tradition of the eighteenth and nineteenth century; I am most fortunate to have their interest, talent, and collaboration in my work.

To create a jeweled object requires many years of experience—by the artist, the jewelers, and the setter of the stones. One must be aware of what has been created in the span of six thousand years, as the history of goldsmithing is a very long one, and despite the ravages of war and time we are fortunate to have many marvels to study and admire. For example, in doing my nautilus shell cup, it was important to know how similar shells had been mounted in Augsburg, Nürnberg, and in the goldsmith centers of Antwerp in the sixteenth century, so that mine would be original and different.

A keen sense of scale is very important in designing anything, whether large or small. Particularly is this so in creating a small exquisite jewel. A lovely gold box or precious bibelot should give delight to the eye at a glance. One observes in a jewel not only design and proportion, but also the workmanship, the skill with which the diamonds are set, and the various finishes given the metal—shiny, satin, florentine, or nugget. These can be studied and admired as one does the brush strokes and techniques of a great painting.

It is almost impossible to set a price on the time and effort spent on one of these gold and jeweled pieces. The jeweler must not be rushed if he is to achieve the best effect. A great many of the processes and techniques of antiquity are lost to us today. For example, the skillful carvings in hard stones and ivory of the early Chinese masters, the work in coral of seventeenth- and eighteenth-century Italy, and the small gold figures and cameos of the ancient world—these are all impossible to reproduce now. Very fine granulation—the soldering of thousands of minute gold beads to a small surface as practiced by the early Greeks and Etruscans—is a lost art. The great enamels of the Renaissance and the fifteenth-century Germans, and the Fabergé enamels of the nineteenth century, are just now being revived and practiced in jewelry. Though some magnificent gold boxes and menodiers are being made and designed, yet none can equal the small boxes of Adrien Vachette of Paris, and Johann Neuber at Dresden, working in the eighteenth century. Hardstone and mosaic inlay is a specialty much too difficult to practice in these hasty times. However, the art and skill of the modern lapidary and diamond cutter surpass that of any previous age, and the setting of gems has now been so perfected that some stones can be invisibly set with no metal showing around the stone.

Popular in the cabinets of the wealthy Renaissance collectors were such rareties in Europe as ostrich eggs, rhinoceros horns, nautilus shells, coconut shells, brought back largely by sailors. Ecclesiastical relics, such as the bones of saints, bits of fabric, pieces of the True Cross, were housed in magnificent and elaborate monstrances of crystal and gold. During the fifteenth and sixteenth centuries there was a revival of collecting precious objects, cameos, and small statues and fragments from the classical period of Greece and Rome. Rock crystal, jasper, heliotrope, and lapis lazuli were much sought after to decorate cups and chalices. All these were inspiration for the various court jewelers and were mounted most elaborately in settings of jewels, gold, silver-gilt, and enamel.

My collection demonstrates the same basic themes. During my travels I have found rare small statues and carvings in bronze, gold, ivory, coral, turquoise, malachite, lapis lazuli, and amber. For my early Greek coins in gold and silver, I have designed stands of ivory wands from India, set in gold and topped by pear-shaped emeralds. A small gold statue of the eighteenth century from Nepal is set under a pagoda of black pearls, gold, and diamonds. At the covered bazaar in

Istanbul my wife and I acquired a small ivory temple with columns. A Byzantine dome and statue topped this carving; removing this I had a pure Greek Tholos in ivory. Under this I put a gold statue mounted on a large topaz, giving the right scale and a classical effect. A fragment of shell found at St. James's Beach in Barbados is mounted with gold seaweed, and supports a coral mermaid from eighteenth-century Naples. To gain decorative value and importance I placed my ancient Greek bronze bull and bronze foot on bases of lapis lazuli and gold. Each of my pieces is a combination of rare objects found in my travels.

When I wished a bibelot to have a look of the eighteenth century, briolette-cut diamonds were used. This cut, giving the effect of a brilliant drop of water, is obsolete; there is too much waste in cutting a diamond this way. It was most popular in the time of the Czars of Russia and Sultans of Turkey in the eighteenth or nineteenth century. The diamonds I have used came from an old necklace belonging to the last Sultan, Abd-Ul-Hamid II.

I hope the examples pictured in this book will give the reader a small part of the pleasure I have had in designing and making these pieces.

GEORGE W. HEADLEY
La Belle Farm
Lexington, Kentucky
May 26, 1965

Introduction

The art of combining goldsmithwork with jewels and semi-precious stones has a tradition that brightened the very early centuries of our civilization, when men discovered the delight of availing themselves of gold, silver, and gems or minerals of many kinds and colors for their personal adornment and the decoration of the implements of their daily lives, as well as of their ritualistic vessels.

An ancient Sumerian love song translated by Professor Samuel Kramer reveals, for example, the appreciation of lapis-lazuli.

> "Because I uttered it, because I uttered it,
>   the Lord gave me a gift.
> Because I uttered the *Allari*-song,
>   the Lord gave me a gift,
> A pendant of gold, a seal of lapis-lazuli,
>   the Lord gave me as a gift."

During the first centuries of the Christian era and thereafter, gold and precious stones were prized for the enhancing of ritual objects. As Anatole Frolow states, Saint Paul wished all liturgical vessels to surpass in splendor those that served in the temple of Solomon. George Pisides, writing in the seventh century, says that "the contemplation of precious stones directs our thoughts toward God."

The Abbot Suger, living in the eleventh century, wrote that dwelling on the beauty of multi-colored gems affords transport to a region from which one may reach the celestial world. Another religious writer considered the sapphire a spiritual element on which to engrave the figure of Our Lord, since it placed Him in the blue of the Heavens. The amethyst has long been considered a fitting stone for the episcopal ring.

Also, at a comparatively early date, there began the custom of setting cameos and intaglios of ancient origin in contemporary settings, a mode in which Mr. George Headley has achieved many exhilarating effects.

It was during the early Byzantine period that this vogue for setting older cameos and intaglios in contemporary settings began, and it continued on through the life of the empire. Illustrating it is the great treasure house of late antique hardstone carvings in the collection of Byzantine liturgical vessels in the Treasury of San Marco in Venice.

During the last half of the first millennium of our era in Western Europe, the so-called "Dark Ages," early mineral carvings were enhanced by contemporary settings in many instances. The Franks and the Merovingians followed this tradition, as did the Carolingians, the most illustrious example of which is the great cameo of Augustus set in the center of the gold cross of King Lothair at Aachen. Following this inspiration, the Ottonians set an early Byzantine intaglio in the crown of the Holy Roman Emperor, shown now in the Schatzkammer in Vienna.

The Church has preserved a great many cult objects from the Middle Ages which incorporate early mineral carvings. Doubtless there existed, also, an equal number of secular objects similarly designed in gold and silver, but being secular, these were more quickly reduced in times of need to mere expedient value.

The Renaissance, with its quickening interest in antiquity and in the collection and preservation of classical objects, gave fresh impetus to the desire for mounting ancient treasures in newly designed settings. Members of the Medici family were particularly active in collecting art creations of the past and incorporating them in settings of that time; some, such as Francisco di Medici, working directly with artists, suggested designs for mountings and gave support generally. The Museo degli Argenti in the Pitti Palace in Florence houses a small portion of the Medici Collection formed during the fifteenth through the eighteenth centuries. Here, some of the late antique and Byzantine ritual vessels in hardstone mounted in Renaissance settings of gold and silver rival the Byzantine ones in the Treasury of San Marco.

Obviously the movement was not confined to Italy, but was followed elsewhere during the Renaissance and through the eighteenth century; the courts of Europe contributed richly to the mounting of antique hardstone carvings in newly designed settings of gold, silver, and enamel with precious stones. In France, Francis I, Henry IV, Louis XIV and his son, the Dauphin, Louis XV, Louis XVI, and Marie Antoinette added to the royal storehouse of such treasures, many of which may be seen today in the Louvre. The Hapsburgs left a truly magnificent array of objects, now in the museums of Vienna; the Wittelsbachs of Bavaria, those in the Schatzkammer in Munich; the Danish Royal House, those in the Rosenborg Castle in Copenhagen; the House of Saxony, those in the Grunes Gewölbe in Dresden; and the Tsars and Tsarinas of Russia, those in the Oruzheinaya Museum in the Moscow Kremlin, in the Hermitage in Leningrad, and in many imperial palaces.

The Church, of course, has contributed to the traditional remounting of antiques in new and harmonious settings. One of the most startlingly beautiful is a monstrance in the Treasure Room of the Convent of the Loreto in Prague. Literally thousands of diamonds, left by a patroness of the convent, lend brilliance to the faultless design of the great Baroque architect, Fischer von Erlach, who left so many palaces in Vienna.

American museums have rarely collected such objects. Usually they have received them as gifts from distinguished private collectors such as J. P. Morgan, Henry Walters, and Joseph Widener. It is a sophisticated taste for which Americans seem not, as yet, completely prepared, insofar as collecting is concerned.

Mr. George Headley is today one of the few designers of goldsmithwork and jewelry, if not the only one engaged in carrying on the tradition now nearly two thousand years old. In looking over these pages illustrating his work, one recalls the pleasure experienced in European museums and the delight of seeing ancient objects mounted in the designs of later centuries.

In all of these museums, Mr. Headley has studied and obviously been inspired to combine his remarkable talent for design with the foremost goldsmiths of today working under his direction. In so doing he has not only enlivened a great tradition but brought to it a fresh vision, and achieved in his exquisite designs a unique and piquant delicacy.

MARVIN C. ROSS
Hillwood, Washington, D.C.
October 22, 1965

Illustrations

The photographs of the objects are by Stone and Langley.

I. BIRD CAGE

A Chinese figure carved in Persian turquoise is seated on a cushion of lapis lazuli in an 18 karat gold cage adorned with pear-shaped sapphires and round diamonds. Height 7⅛ inches.

JEWELER: *Ernst Just, Charles Vaillant Inc., New York*

PLATE I

II. DAPHNE

The figure and the blossoms of the 18 karat gold tree are carved in antique Italian coral and encrusted with diamonds. The rock is of soufre. Height 7½ inches.

JEWELER: *Ernst Just, Charles Vaillant Inc., New York*

PLATE II

III. UNDERSEA MOVEMENT

A Japanese ivory fish studded with emeralds and sapphires is mounted on gold coral set on natural coral. Gold, sapphire, and turquoise starfish and sea anemones complete the composition. The base is black marble. Height 6¾ inches.

JEWELER: *David Webb Inc., New York*

PLATE III

IV. COMPOSITION WITH THREE ANCIENT GREEK GOLD FIGURES

The three gold figures come from a Greek child's necklace of 400 B.C. They are mounted with gold granulation duck heads, topaz, and pearls. The entire composition rests on a black lacquer base. Height 6¼ inches, including base.

Mounted by Charles Vaillant Inc., New York

PLATE IV

V. COLLECTION OF ANCIENT GREEK COINS IN GOLD AND SILVER (ONE OF A PAIR)

The coins hang from the gold arms of a stand fashioned out of ivory and gold, and topped by a pear-shaped emerald. The teak base contains a drawer. Height 7½ inches.

JEWELER: *Werner Schirrmeister, Charles Vaillant Inc., New York*

PLATE V

VI. GODDESS FLORA

An antique Venetian figure in malachite is mounted on a rough malachite base. The canopy of 18 karat gold has vines of blue enamel morning glories and is topped with diamonds and pear-shaped sapphires. Height 5¾ inches.

JEWELER: *Ernst Just, Charles Vaillant Inc., New York*

PLATE VI

VII. CHALICE OF NEPTUNE

Mythological figures and diamond-spouting dolphins of antique Italian coral cavort around gold rocks, seaweed in 18 karat chased gold, pearl shell, pearls, and briolette diamonds. Height 8¼ inches.

JEWELER: *Ernst Just, Charles Vaillant Inc., New York*

PLATE VII

VIII. JEWELED, JADE, AND ONYX WATCH BIBELOT

A delicately carved Ching Dynasty female figure of pale lavender jade has touches of green marking the fish in her hand and on her pole. She stands on an onyx base adorned with gold and diamond seaweed. In the center of the base is a platinum, coral enamel, ruby, and diamond watch mounted on white jade, which is suspended from the seaweed above. Height 10½ inches.

JEWELER: *Charles Vaillant Inc., New York*

PLATE VIII

IX. ANCIENT GREEK BRONZES

Two sculptures, a foot of 400 B.C. and a bull of 800 B.C., are mounted on bases of lapis lazuli and gold ropes. Height including bases: foot, 2¾ inches; bull, 3⅛ inches.

JEWELER: *Charles Vaillant Inc., New York*

PLATE IX

X. JADE VASE AND WATCH BIBELOT

The Ching Dynasty vase is of white jade. The watch is also white jade set in platinum, gold, enamel, rubies, and diamonds. The timepiece hangs flexibly from a ruby and gold ribbon. The base is lacquered wood. Height 6¾ inches.

Mounted by Charles Vaillant Inc., New York

PLATE X

XI. BYZANTINE SAINT MICHAEL

This is a copy of Saint Michael from the Treasury of Saint Mark's basilica in Venice. It is engraved in 22 karat gold and adorned with translucent enamel. Height 3½ inches, width 3⅛ inches.

JEWELER: *Zolotas, Athens*

PLATE XI

XII. NIRVANA IN THAILAND

The base and cover are from a seventeenth-century Siamese box in pure gold and enamel. The figure is a Chinese carving in gem turquoise. The stand and supporting rods are of gold, turquoise, and diamonds. The composition is in three sections, and may be made into a cup if desired. Height 6¾ inches.

Supports by Ernst Just, Charles Vaillant Inc., New York

PLATE XII

XIII. SHELL WITH MERMAID

An antique coral mermaid from Naples rests on gold seaweed which sprouts from the center of a shell-fragment from Barbados. The whole piece is mounted in gold seaweed. Coral bud-like forms hang from the seaweed. Height 6¼ inches.

JEWELER: *Charles Vaillant Inc., New York*

PLATE XIII

XIV. SEESAW OF LIFE

Antique French gold figures balance on a gold plank hung with ruby drops. In the center, the emerald leaves of a tree encircle a ruby heart. The amethyst and agate base is adorned with gold flowers. The piece is set in 18 karat gold. Height 3¼ inches.

JEWELER: *Ernst Just, Charles Vaillant Inc., New York*

PLATE XIV

XV. EIGHTEENTH-CENTURY ITALIAN URN

An antique Italian ivory urn is adorned with a gold and diamond bird and gold leaves on which flexible briolette diamonds hang. The urn is mounted on an onyx and gold base. Height 6¾ inches.

JEWELER: *Charles Vaillant Inc., New York*

PLATE XV

XVI. NEPALI FIGURE IN PAGODA

An eighteenth-century gold god figure on a Lion from Nepal is set in a pagoda of gold, diamonds, and black pearls. The base is of abalone pearl. Height 4⅞ inches.

JEWELER: *Charles Vaillant Inc., New York*

PLATE XVI

XVII. OBELISK OF THE MERMAID

An antique English carving of a mermaid in malachite is set on a Venetian crystal obelisk, which is mounted in gold and malachite. Height 9¾ inches.

JEWELER: *Werner Schirrmeister, Charles Vaillant Inc., New York*

PLATE XVII

XVIII A. MASK OF BACCHUS

A seventeenth-century Italian coral mask of the mythological god of wine, his eyes set with emeralds, is mounted with coral branches on a base of gold and onyx. The god's characteristic motif is seen in the gold grape vine set in the back of his mask and in the clusters of gold grapes and leaves which adorn the base. Height 4½ inches.

JEWELER: *Romolo Grassi, Milan*

XVIII B. PAIR OF CORAL PUTTI

Two playful coral putti are mounted on matching amber and gold bases. Heights 3¾ inches and 3¼ inches.

JEWELER: *Charles Vaillant Inc., New York*

54

PLATE XVIII

XIX. IVORY AND GOLD CANDLESTICKS

The candlesticks of ivory are adorned with gold and diamond leaves and gold birds from whose beaks hang pear-shaped diamonds. Height 3¼ inches.

JEWELER: *Charles Vaillant Inc., New York*

PLATE XIX

XX. CARVING OF "HO KSEIN KU"

This Chinese coral figure is mounted with diamonds, onyx, turquoise, and ivory. The composition is topped with a pin from Cartier's. The base is onyx. The backdrop is in gold mesh. Height 6⅛ inches.

Assembled by Charles Vaillant Inc., New York

PLATE XX

XXI. PAIR OF CHINESE PRIESTS

Two Chinese aquamarine figures are set in cornucopia-shaped forms of chased 22 karat gold and briolette diamonds. The bases are black onyx. Heights 2¾ inches.

JEWELER: *Ernst Just, Charles Vaillant Inc., New York*

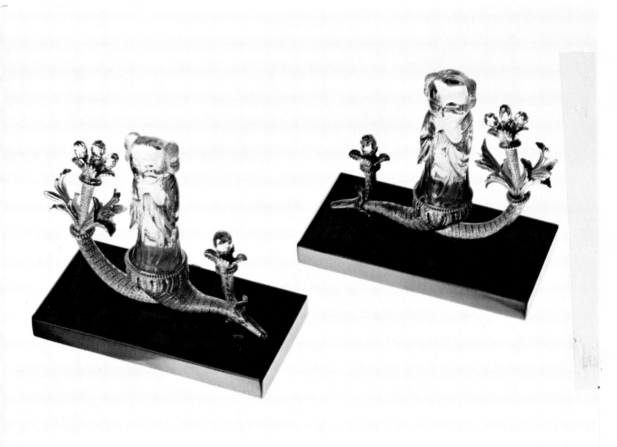

PLATE XXI

XXII. BOY ON A DRAGON

The figure of a boy in 18 karat gold sits astride an antique coral Chinese dragon, which is mounted on a soapstone base. The boy's wand is adorned with imperial jade and his cape, with flexible diamonds. Height 7⅛ inches, length 7¾ inches.

JEWELER: *Romolo Grassi, Milan*

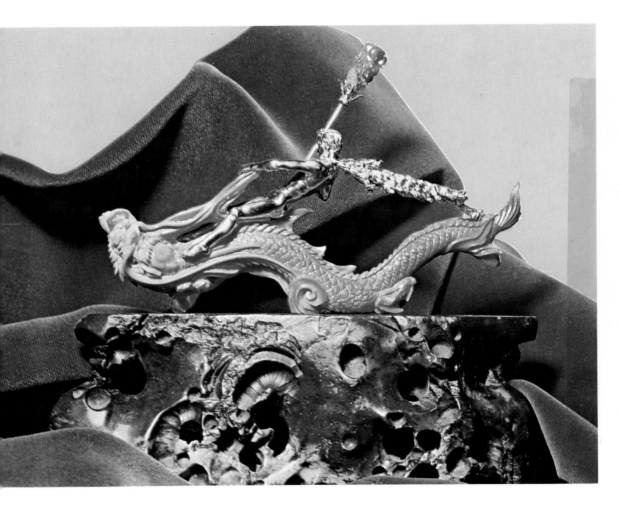

PLATE XXII

XXIII. OBELISKS WITH PUTTI

A crown of diamonds, emeralds, and rubies tops the center of this composition of lapis lazuli, gold, and baroque pearl. Three gold angels play musical instruments. Height 3½ inches.

Assembled by Werner Schirrmeister, Charles Vaillant Inc., New York

PLATE XXIII

XXIV. CLOCK WITH SEVEN HAND FETISHES

Seven semi-precious stone hands from Brazil are mounted in gold flames around a gold clock. The base is onyx. Height 3¾ inches.

Mounted by David Webb Inc., New York

66

PLATE XXIV

XXV. JEWELED AND 18 KARAT GOLD CLOCK BIBELOT

The coral elephant has trappings of gold bamboo, tassels, and pearls. A watch in coral, diamonds, and enamel swings from the center of the howdah. The base is of lapis lazuli, gold, and cabochon emeralds. A blackamoor holds a fan of emerald jade. Height 5 inches.

JEWELER: *Ernst Just, Charles Vaillant Inc., New York*

PLATE XXV

XXVI. GREEK IVORY THOLOS

An ivory temple from Istanbul is topped with six ivory finials, and decorated with gold beading. In the center of the temple is a gold statue of classical motif, which is mounted on a topaz, gold, and diamond base. Height 6½ inches.

JEWELER: *Charles Vaillant Inc., New York*

PLATE XXVI

XXVII. GOLD BOX

This gold box bears an undersea design, which is set in tortoiseshell enamel, and bordered with panels of seaweed and fish. Height ⅞ inches, width 3⅛ inches, length 4½ inches.

JEWELER: *Romolo Grassi, Milan*

PLATE XXVII

XXVIII. GOLD BOX IN THE RENAISSANCE TASTE

The sides are decorated with six rare eighteenth-century carvings of animal heads in coral. On top, three putti struggle with a snake. Coral columns and green enamel vines also adorn the box. Height 2½ inches, diameter 5½ inches.

JEWELER: *Romolo Grassi, Milan*

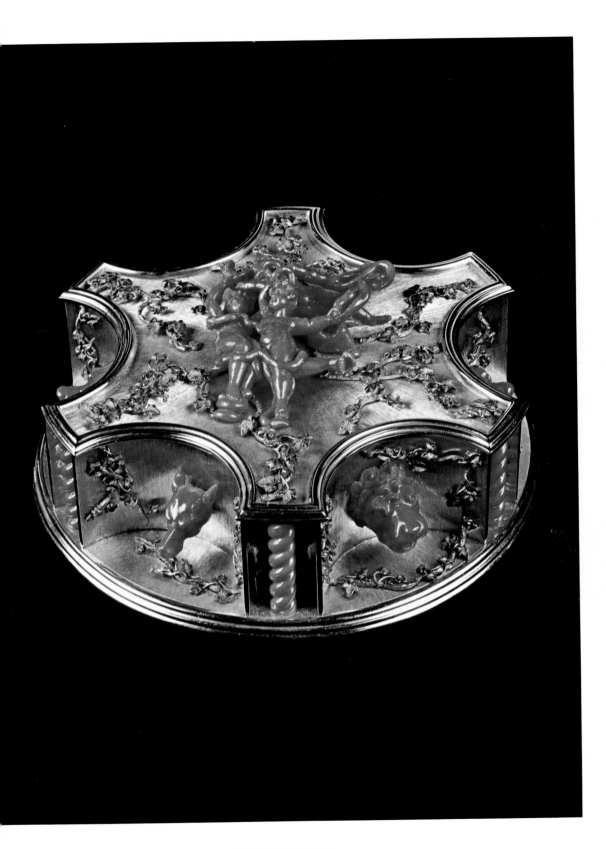

PLATE XXVIII

XXIX. GOLD AND ENAMEL CIGARETTE BOX

The frieze-like design on this cigarette box was taken from a Greek vase in the Prado Museum in Madrid. Height 2¼ inches, length 6 inches.

JEWELER: *Romolo Grassi, Milan*

PLATE XXIX

XXX. BIRD'S NEST BOX

A Swiss wood-carving of a walnut is decorated with gold and diamond birds and transformed into a golden nest, replete with turquoise eggs. Three canary diamond butterflies complete the composition. Height 2 ¼ inches.

Box made by Charles Vaillant Inc., New York

PLATE XXX

XXXI. GOLD BOX WITH FIGURE OF NEPTUNE

A gold figure of the sea-god brandishes his trident of gold. He stands on a gold rock surrounded by enamel waves, gold sea shells, and clusters of jewels. The composition is mounted on a vermeil box. Height 4 inches, width 3½ inches, length 5½ inches.

JEWELER: *Romolo Grassi, Milan; Box by Tiffany & Co.*

PLATE XXXI

XXXII A. PAIR OF ANTIQUE CORAL FIGURES

The figures are mounted on bases of malachite and gold. Height 4¼ inches.

JEWELER: *Charles Vaillant Inc., New York*

XXXII B. GOLD CIGARETTE BOX

The box is in chased gold with borders of grape vines. The antique coral figure from Naples holds a dove. Height 4¼ inches.

JEWELER: *Romolo Grassi, Milan*

PLATE XXXII

Notes and Sketches

[I] *In all my collecting of bibelots, done in various stones, I still hadn't seen any turquoise good enough in color and carving that I wanted to mount in gold. I love the color and was most desirous of adding some of it to my collection. One day there came a long-distance call from the New York jeweler David Webb; a dealer had brought in a pair of Chinese carvings for him to see. I was delighted to acquire them. When they arrived they were indeed superb; being crisply carved and of perfect color. This design shows a very elegant lady sitting on a cushion of lapis lazuli. She is in a bird cage of gold, diamonds, and pear-shaped sapphires. The dark blue of the sapphires and lapis lazuli and the pale blue-green of the turquoise make a lovely combination. The piece hangs from a gold cord.*

[II] *This bibelot was begun when I found a beautiful example of the rock soufre in a shop on the rue du Bac in Paris. A year later I was fortunate in buying a large collection of antique Italian carvings from a family in Naples. This collection was formed during hundreds of years. The coral woman used here seemed ready to float into space. I designed a gold tree with blossoms of coral and diamonds to bring the coral and the rock together. In this bibelot the two most important things are the proper scale and relation to each other of the three elements used, and the modeling and chasing of the gold tree.*

II   II

[v] *The ivory columns were originally handles for feather fans from India. They are used here, with gold arms coming out from them, to hang my collection of ancient Greek gold and silver coins. The bases are black lacquer and contain a small drawer in which are kept data and dates relating to each coin. A cabochon emerald tops each stand.*

[VII] *There have been many cups and chalices made around the nautilus shell. Before designing this one I made a careful study of the ones done in the past. Two coral Italian carvings of undersea gods and dolphins, from a collection in Naples, give color and design. The dolphins spill forth diamond water. Chased gold undersea plants flow over gold rocks, then are pressed into a column to support the shell. Various branches flow out at the top and wind around the shell. From these branches hang pearls and briolette diamonds. The modeling of the gold and the hand chasing are superb, and took four months to execute.*

V

VII

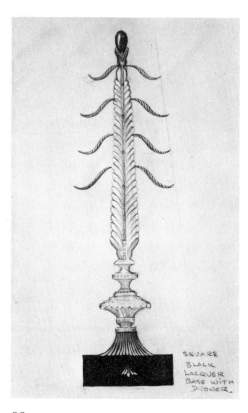

SQUARE
BLACK
LACQUER
BASE WITH
DROWER.

88

[XIII] *The shell-fragment used here I found on St. James's beach in Barbados. For a time it was a model used in one of my paintings, then it went into my shell collection. Upon looking through my collection of coral, I decided the mermaid would complement the shell. These two were locked together with modeled and chased gold sea plants. Since this photograph was taken, the piece has been put on an oval base of malachite.*

[XVII] *Located near the British Museum is the Cameo Shop. This mermaid in malachite was in a pin that I found there. The smoky crystal I had made in Venice. Two fluted gold shells with balls of malachite hold the obelisk. The finial is in gold and malachite. Here, again, the scale and relation of things to each other is most important in the final object.*

XVII

[XXI] *A few months after acquiring this lovely pair of Chinese figures in aquamarine, I decided how to best mount them. It would have been too easy to design something for them based on examples of Chinese design. The gold work is certainly oriental in feeling, but of no particular country. The briolette diamonds used here are important enough for the size of the large aquamarine figures. They give the effect of little lights. The black onyx bases give strength and pull the whole effect together.*

[XXII] *I have a third-century Roman agate ring engraved with Eros riding a dolphin. Owning a fine carving of a Chinese dragon in coral, I began to model the boy. A boy on a dragon would be a little different. What a difficult time it was to model, in detail, such a small figure with his flowing cape. Many times his arms or legs would break off. When I finally had him just right, I flew to Milan with the wax carefully packed. In the Poldi-Pezzoli Museum there is a wonderful bronze Greek head of a boy. Giving Mr. Grassi a photograph of this head, I asked him to put it on my boy riding the dragon. The rider is holding a wand topped by a carving in imperial jade; his cape has a fringe of small flexible diamonds. The base is a carving in soapstone from China.*

XXI

XXII

[xxv] *My wife had three small possessions that worried me—they were lovely, but never used. Her mother's pearl hat pin, an old-fashioned coral and diamond watch on a black cord, and a charming coral carving of an elephant. In putting the three together in this design, I created a surprise for her. The howdah on the elephant is in gold bamboo and pearls; from its center the watch swings backward and forward to show the time. The elephant boy holds a wand of carved emerald jade. The base is lapis lazuli and gold, studded with cabochon emeralds. The small tassels that hang from the gold and diamond elephant blanket are flexible. The hat pin tops it all.*

[xxx] *The idea of making this Swiss carving of a walnut into a box came to me in the middle of the night. I drew the two gold and diamond birds building a nest and the three canary diamond butterflies. The next question was where to put the nest. By cutting the walnut in half and hollowing it out, I had space for the nest. When it opens and one sees the turquoise eggs, it is a surprise. The textures of wood and gold are very pleasing together. This is just another example of a souvenir of one's travels that, with a little imagination, turns out to be a more interesting object.*

xxx

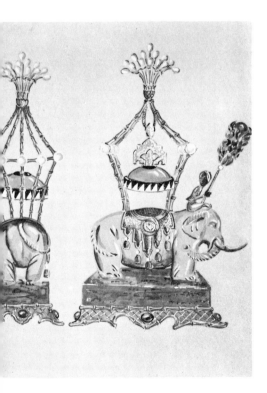

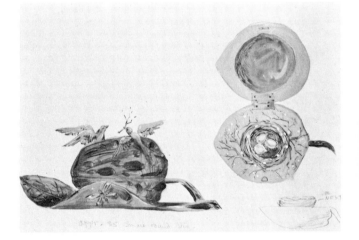

[XXXI] *My first design for the ornament on this gold box was a girl fishing, with a wave in enamel breaking over gold rocks and shells (Sketch No. 1). It needed more height, I decided, so I drew the bearded Neptune with trident, which is shown in sketches 2 and 3. The enamel wave ends in diamond foam. This, I feel, is a wonderful example of the jeweler's art of today. The texture of the rocks is different from that used on the shells; while Neptune alone is in shiny gold.*

No. 2

No. 1

No. 3